HE SPENDS

She Spends

PARTICIPANT'S GUIDE

HE SPENDS
She Spends

Why God Wants You To Live For Free

JOHN H. PUTNAM

Fedd Books
P.O. Box 341973
Austin, TX 78734
www.thefeddagency.com

Published in association with The Fedd Agency, Inc., a literary agency.

Unless otherwise indicated, Scripture quotations marked [NIV] are taken from the *Holy Bible, New International Version®*, NIV®. Copyright © 1973, 1978, 1984, 2011 by Biblica, Inc.™ Used by permission of Zondervan. All rights reserved worldwide. www.zondervan.com. The "NIV" and "New International Version" are trademarks registered in the United States Patent and Trademark Office by Biblica, Inc.

Scripture quotations marked [NLT] are taken from the *Holy Bible*, New Living Translation, copyright ©1996, 2004, 2007, 2013 by Tyndale House Foundation. Used by permission of Tyndale House Publishers, Inc., Carol Stream, Illinois 60188. All rights reserved.

Scripture quotations marked [KJV] are from T*he Authorized (King James) Version*. Rights in the Authorized Version in the United Kingdom are vested in the Crown. Reproduced by permission of the Crown's patentee, Cambridge University Press.

Special thank you to www.openbible.com and www.biblegateway.com which I used in my research and preparation

ISBN: 978-1-943217-16-8
eISBN: 978-1-943217-17-5

Cover and Interior Design by: Lauren Hall

Printed in the United States of America

First Edition 15 14 13 10 09 / 10 9 8 7 6 5 4 3 2 1

c o n t e n t s

PLEASE READ THIS FIRST..........................xiii

WEEK 1..........................11
It's Not About the Money
Starting Together

WEEK 2..........................29
Living Free
Wanting More

WEEK 3..........................43
Taking Control
Getting What You Asked For

WEEK 4..........................57
We're Not Alone
Less is More

WEEK 5..........................71
Recapturing Life
Starting Together...Again

Welcome to *He Spends, She Spends Participant's Guide*. You might be starting on this journey reading through the book while participating in a group or individual study at the same time or you might have read the *He Spends, She Spends* book and decided you want to go deeper. Either way, my prayer is that we are starting a conversation that will help you begin thinking more about what is behind your money moments and taking action on your financial choices from God's perspective.

Our money moments involve real life, real choices, real money, and real consequences. As with the book, the questions and activities around these moments in the participant's guide don't really get into the actual dollars and cents of your finances. We aren't offering you budgeting spreadsheets or calculators. Instead, we are going to work through some self-examination and prayerful consideration of why you use your money the way you do. *What really happens before you make a spending decision? Do behaviors play a role? What about your past? What do you really believe? How about your own personal desires? And what about those around you? Are you shutting your spouse out of money decisions when they could be your partner? Are your friend's lives impacting how you view your own?* These and many other questions will be part of the exploration of you and your money.

You may know what the Bible says about money and you may

understand how to handle your money in a practical fashion, but that does not guarantee success in your financial life because there is a lot going on, in and around, your finances that can be a barrier between you and God's plans for your life. I believe it's because you may not fully understand why you make the choices you do and the factors that contribute to those choices.

This participant's guide is a companion for the "why to" found in the book. We will dig into the depths of your choices and we will explore your silent partners that shape your financial choices. You will gain new insights and take fresh practical steps to bring clarity and unity to your plans. But most of all, we pray you will draw closer to Christ and away from the distracting influences around your money.

Each week you will be presented a series of questions and situations that will follow a simple pattern of *exploration, conversation, prayer,* and *reflection*:

- **QUESTION***: I like to think about the questions in this guide as "thought leaders." Every question is like a short journey that will take you to new place, if only for a moment. And in any new place there are new sights and new thoughts.*
- **CONVERSATION***: The questions are thorough, but I truly believe that the real progress from the questions is found in what God will reveal in what arises for you around the questions. I pray these questions lead your thoughts in new conversations with each other and with God.*
- **ANSWER***: As you are writing your answers, I pray God will be talking with you, guiding you, and encouraging you. There is space provided to note your responses, the highlights of your conversations, and additional space for notes at the end of each week's lesson.*

- **SCRIPTURE**: *At the end of each question is a scripture for you to locate in your Bible and write in the space provided. This is a critical part of this guide so please embrace this powerful step. Think about the perspectives found in the scripture in relation to the question and your responses.*
- **PRAYER & ACTION**: *Take the opportunity to pray the scripture back to God as you ask Him to reveal new thoughts and new actions that He desires for you. Write these down. Something supernatural happens to our heart when we read God's word, write God's word, and then pray God's word back to Him.*
- **REFLECTION:** *Finally, take a moment to reflect upon the week's lesson, read the prayer together, and add your own prayers and prayer requests from the week. Please share them with the group if God so leads. As you choose to share your financial situations, battles and victories, it will create an open oneness in your group—you'll see God work in fresh new ways, love and respect will build, the power of comparison will begin to erode, and many of the enemy's schemes will cease to take hold.*

One last note: While most of the examples and instructions speak to husbands and wives and the challenges they face individually and as a couple who are sharing in financial decisions, the truths represented still apply to those who are single and trying to get a grip on their finances. If you don't have a spouse, consider how you would want to deal with your financial issues today. You may be married in the future, or you may remain single, either way, this guide will help you build a solid foundation.

As you read through the book and participant's guide, there is a lot you will learn about yourself and what drives and impacts your financial decisions and your actions. I pray those discoveries will not only help strengthen your financial situation, but also strengthen your relationship with each other, and with God. I believe if only one question each week creates a closer walk with Christ and each other, it will be life changing. It's been said that "money doesn't come with instructions," but I believe God's word provides exactly that and so much more. He is

> *Something supernatural happens to our heart when we read God's word, write God's word and then pray God's word back to Him.*

the *question* and the *answer* to all—the Alpha and Omega—it all begins and ends with Him.

week **one**

We will begin by looking at what motivates you in your financial choices. This week is about discovering and digging into the filters of justification, explanation, and rationalization that so often cloud our judgment; it is about looking at our habits honestly to find what directs them. You may find some of it challenging, but it is crucial to keep going so you can move on to an improved financial future, living for free, further away from the stress and worry that comes from the consequences of our choices.

(Genesis 1:27)
(Genesis 1:28-29, 31)

1 In the book, I opened Chapter 1 with a story of a personal experience where I woke up early with worry—a mild panic even—on my mind. I had made some financial choices that were affecting my peace of mind and my sleep. Think back on a recent "worry wake up call" and let's begin to uncover some trends.

- *What thoughts or situations ran through your mind that created worry?*

- *How did that anxiety and restlessness affect the rest of your day, your work, or your relationships?*

- *What are some things you might do to prevent money from having this influence on you?*

- *Write Matthew 6:33-34.*

> *Comparison destroys contentment, then creates it.*

2 We all tend to romanticize the past and gloss over the unpleasant stuff. We forget the reality of our struggles. But, there are truths in our ability to accept simplicity and live within our means that could still apply as your situation changes and your ability to afford more expands.

- *If it were possible to get it back, what would be the one experience you would love to have again from those early days? Could you create a similar experience today?*

- *What made that time special and what was it about your perspective that made it possible to see what you had as enough?*

- How does that memory affect the way you might use the level of resources you now have?

- Write John 14:26.

3 Throughout the book, I have repeated a statement that has two distinct messages. *"Comparison destroys contentment, then creates it."* I want us to dig into the first part now. Comparison is the death of contentment because it makes us look at what has been good in our lives and suddenly find fault with it. Sometimes comparing yourself to those with less and those with more have very different effects on our contentment.

- Note some of the ways you have compared your situation to others recently. How may it have affected your contentment?

- Do you expect God to treat everyone the same? Why or why not?

- Write John 21:21-22.

> The world's **better**
> never quite measures
> up to God's **best**.

4 The second part of the statement, "*Comparison destroys contentment, then creates it,*" addresses what happens to contentment when it arrives at its destination and looks around for justification and approval. An example might be, "If they're a Christian family and living in that house, driving that car, etc., then it must be okay for me, too." The feeling of accomplishment, a feeling of having arrived, is usually short-lived because if you compared yourself once, you're likely to do it again.

- *What are some dangers of looking at the actions and choices of others to support the decisions you are making or that you want to make?*

- *Describe how you may have used comparison to justify a choice. Then list some tangible ways to combat this common trap.*

-*Write Philippians 4:12.*

> *Busy makes you plan.*
> *Stuff slows you down.*
> *Money can be an isolator.*

5 Now, think about the items you already have and may want to upgrade. These items may be the same goals that others dream of achieving. Note how easily you can experience a reversal of perception just by a change in perspective.

- Rewrite some of those comparison items from Question #3 and note how a perspective might be reversed if someone else were comparing themselves to you.

- Write Titus 2:6-7.

> *Money moments can hide what's really going on—unknown, unobserved, untouched.*

6 There is a little bitty word that packs a really big punch: *IF.* "If I could just get a little bit ahead in the race . . . ," "If I get that raise . . . ," "If we had a bigger house . . . ," "If we just had more money . . ." So often, we get distracted into imagining the future instead of living in the present. We imagine destinations or events ahead of us that we believe will affect our financial lives for the better. Consider how you may be playing the *IF* game in your own life.

- *What areas of your life do you hope these* IF *destinations will improve, and what results will they provide?*

- *If you never arrive at your next* IF *destination, list a few specific truths for your contentment right where you are.*

- *Write James 4:13-17.*

7 The *IF* game can look a lot like striving and one of the ways God may use to help us recognize this is creating a barrier in our lives is through a strategic interruption. Imagine how you would react to an actual reversal in your situation by a strategic interruption such as the loss of a job, a health issue, an unexpected job offer, etc.

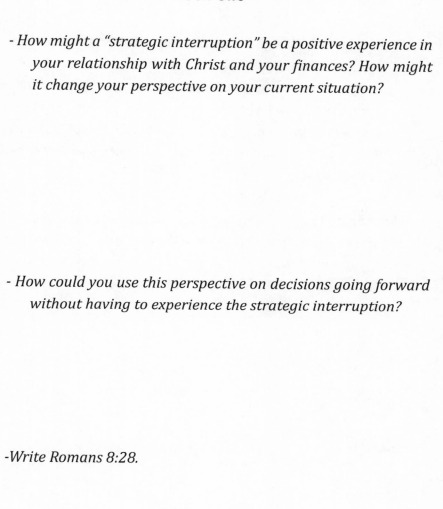

- How might a "strategic interruption" be a positive experience in your relationship with Christ and your finances? How might it change your perspective on your current situation?

- How could you use this perspective on decisions going forward without having to experience the strategic interruption?

-Write Romans 8:28.

8 Most families make financial choices with a dangerous blindness to the forces that impact those decisions. In our money moments, we can be frozen by fears, burdened by regrets, distracted by beliefs, derailed by behaviors, and challenged by perspective.

- *Using these money moments, let's begin to record some influences on how you approach your money in motion and the ways these limitations are impacting your life. You may have an answer for each moment, or, there may only be specific moments that God wants to reveal to you now. Take your time and pause in prayer as you ask God to reveal himself to you.*

- **Frozen by fears** – *The future can be daunting and we can spend much of our mental and emotional energy concerned about tomorrow. What is it that creates a fear, or burdensome uncertainty, about your financial future, when considering your. . .*

- *Giving*

- *Spending*

- *Saving*

- *Investing*

- *Taxes*

- *Planning*

- *Counsel*

- *Write Isaiah 41:10.*

- **Burdened by regrets** – *Many times we are the last one to forgive ourselves for a past mistake so it continues to have power over us. Are there any past poor financial choices or money mistakes that still affect you today in your. . .*

- *Giving*

- *Spending*

- *Saving*

- *Investing*

- *Taxes*

- *Planning*

- *Counsel*

- *Write Philippians 3:13-15.*

- **Distracted by beliefs** – *Financial beliefs can come from your education, advice from family and friends, and many other sources. List some of your financial beliefs in your...*

- *Giving*

- *Spending*

- *Saving*

- *Investing*

- *Taxes*

- *Planning*

- *Counsel*

- *Write John 20:29.*

- **Derailed by behaviors** – *Bad habits are hard to break and good habits are hard to find! What positive, or negative, financial behaviors, habits or actions do you see repeated in your...*

- *Giving*

- Spending

- Saving

- Investing

- Taxes

- Planning

- Counsel

- Write Matthew 6:19-21.

- **Challenged by perspective** – *A friend once told me that our view of God affects everything we are and everything we do. Keeping this very simple, how does your perspective differ from God's perspective in your. . .*

- Giving

- Spending

- Saving

- Investing

- Taxes

- Planning

- Write Phillipians 4:8.

R E F L E C T I O N

When we start out on our life's journey as adults and in married life, most of us have limited resources and sometimes limited expectations. We learn to be satisfied with what we have because that's all we have. Most of us wind up expanding our relationships rather than expanding wealth. As we settle into our lives, we build community and form other relationships that can offer support and encouragement in the journey.

As time passes, those relationships can present demands, expectations, and comparisons—some positive, some negative— that affect our contentment with our situations and God's plans. As we follow His plans, more sources begin influencing our heads and our hearts. A lot of times we just make bad choices; but there is an enemy who works with his own plans and his own devices and they don't include you following God's plans. Not all of our financial issues can be blamed on the enemy ("the devil made me do it"), but we often make the enemy's job much too easy.

Your old thinking and old actions have gotten you to where you are. To get to where God wants you to go will require a new perspective and new actions. Prayer and action are God's one-two punch. We are beginning a new adventure—one that will free you from your money worries by giving you an abundance of true riches. I can think of no better place to start than "In the beginning"—that brief yet blissful arrival at your own little Garden of Eden.

PRAYER

Thank you for the fresh start each day you give us in our lives in you. It's a special time when we learn to love You and love our spouse in the way You intended. I've often let my mind, my heart, and my actions be overtaken by financial concerns instead of overtaken by my love for You. As lifestyle creeps into our lives, we desire to be in the world but not of it. Please keep us close so we remain united in our journey. You mercifully offer peace in the midst of our busy lives that can only be found in You. Help me to rest in the simplicity and wealth of You and You alone. Amen.

MY PRAYERS
+
PRAYER REQUESTS

notes

notes

week **two**

Last week we began looking at the various trends that drive our financial decisions. This week we are going to consider what it means to live for free—what is true freedom and how does it play out in our lives—and what wanting more from life is supposed to look like. We will have more study to do in uncovering what is behind the choices you make regarding money and will continue on that path addressing the misconceptions around freedom that can cause you to choose poorly and how to get more out of life without increasing your burdens.

(Genesis 2:25)
(Genesis 3:1-5)

1 We all think fondly of times in our lives when we didn't worry too much about providing the necessities of life.

- Try to recall that time and how you felt. Describe that feeling in as much detail as you can.

- In what ways did it affect your work, your personal relationships, and your relationship with God?

- Write Matthew 6:25.

2 We often equate money with freedom, but we're designed to equate freedom with God.

- How does having money affect your worship of God?

- *Does it provide more opportunities for worship or more opportunities for distraction? Explain.*

- *Write Galatians 5:13-14.*

3 Genesis 3:1-5 shows us Eve's encounter with the enemy. We see that he didn't begin by telling her to disobey God. Instead, he simply posed a simple question: "Did God really say that?" He simply planted a seed of doubt, of discontent. Then bent God's words ever so slightly. He does the same thing today.

- *Describe a situation where you would be most vulnerable to the enemy's whisper—Is it a location? An environment? A state of mind? A time of day?*

- *When is your opportune time for him to get you off course?*

- Write Ephesians 6:11.

4 If you have been in church for any length of time you have heard the term "stewardship." We each need to be good stewards of all that God has given us.

- How do you define stewardship and how does it play a role in your life?

- Write 1 Peter 4:10.

5 More isn't automatically bad and less isn't automatically good. Whether you have a lot or a little, it all comes from God. How we use what He has given us determines whether it is a blessing or a burden. In the exercise below we want to begin to identify patterns in the use of your resources, whether they are abundant or limited. Then, we can learn from any patterns, and identify ways you can use them more effectively in the years ahead. Many times, our choices are based on a source that represents a lie. We all know the saying "garbage in, garbage out." Let's make sure we are beginning with truth.

Using the "Financial Forensics" formula on the next pages, and the following worksheet, *retrace one of your own financial choices.*

SOURCE ➡ SENSES ➡ MIND ➡ HEART ➡ CHOICE

FINANCIAL FORENSICS: My CHOICE is/was...	
SOURCE	
SENSE	
MIND	
HEART	

- **SOURCE** – This is where any opportunity, question, or message originates from, and every source has it's own motives and messages. *Where was the message from and how did it get presented to you? Friend, book, magazine, advertising, personal desire, observation, etc.?*

- **SENSES** - God designed our five senses to allow us to see, hear, smell, taste, and touch the world around us that He created. *What senses were involved? Be specific.*

- **MIND** - God has given us the ability to learn, think and reason. Our mind and its respective thoughts are powerful and creative. *What did your head tell you to do?*

- **HEART**- Our hearts house our beliefs and our behaviors. And they hold a multitude of powerful directives. *Did your heart disagree with your head? Which one won?*

- **CHOICE** - After we understand the situation or opportunity at hand, and after we have time to think about it in our minds and wrestle with it in our hearts, it's time to make a choice. *Were you and your spouse in agreement on your choice? Did it take you closer, or further, from God?*

- *Now, start back at the source and identify where you could have seen the "caution flags."*

- *Have you ever you seen caution flags related to a choice and chose to ignore them? Explain.*

- *Write Proverbs 1:32-33.*

6 Praying specifically over your money moments is an important part of making better financial decisions such as the purchase of a new car, how much to invest, what type of products to buy, where to go on vacation, how much do we give, etc.

- *Describe a current financial choice that would benefit from seeking and listening to God's guidance.*

- *Ask yourself how God's word provides support, or warnings, of the situation? Can you find a scripture?*

- *Write 2 Timothy 3:16-17.*

7 Going back to the "Stewardship Specs" we covered in the book, we considered the "Parable of the Talents," identifying the Master/Owner, the Mission/Instructions, the Resources, the Steward, The Choice, the Results/Accountability, and the Reward.

- *Read the following stories aloud and practice identifying the same specs in these other biblical examples of stewardship.*

- *Write about "The Widow with the Jars of Oil" in 2 Kings 4:1-7.*

- *Master/Owner*

- *Mission/Instructions*

- *Resources*

- *Steward*

- *Choice*

- *Results/Accountability*

- *Reward*

- *Enemy/Emotion*

- *Write about "Jesus Feeding the Five Thousand" in Matthew 14: 13-21.*

- *Master/Owner*

- *Mission/Instructions*

- *Resources*

- *Steward*

- *Choice*

- *Results/Accountability*

- *Reward*

- *Enemy/Emotion*

- *Now, take a story from work, or from your family, and see if the same "specs" show up.*

REFLECTION

God wants us to be free; but what we think of as freedom isn't necessarily lasting, true freedom. We have desires of freedom that often don't have eternity in mind. Often, we tend to think money and possessions hold the ability to make us free. We think it means being able to do whatever we want whenever we want. Living free by the world's standards and living free by God's standards often do not look the same. We see our money and possessions from our perspective, but God has an eternal perspective that allows Him to see the impact and burden those things actually have on our lives and on our relationships. True freedom comes when we release our need for control and trust God to lead. Letting go of what we think matters and trusting Him to fill our lives with His spirit and what really matters, our hearts and lives will be enriched for the long run—the only way to truly live for free.

M Y   P R A Y E R

Lord, you had a simple plan for Adam and Eve and I know you have a simple plan for me. Your gifts are always good but I don't always use them the way you have asked. Even your best gifts can be used to imprison me in little, or big ways, when I use them for my purposes and don't follow You. I know I can't love You and money. I often have a foot squarely planted in Your love and the other foot equally firm in the world. I often fall victim to the enemy's traps. Other times I just make my own poor decisions. Help me want You more than I want anything else. Even though my actions may not show it, I pray to have the courage to choose You over all. I want to follow You. I want to live for free. I want to live with abandon with You as my focus. Amen.

MY PRAYERS
+
PRAYER REQUESTS

n o t e s

n o t e s

week **three**

Now that you have a sense of what motivates your financial decisions, you have begun to put your expectations and ideas about freedom in their proper perspective. It's time to examine who (or what) is really controlling the money relationship and getting rid of the worry and feelings of isolation that are affecting your financial situation.

(Genesis 3:1-6)
(Genesis 3:21-24)

1 At some point, the material possessions or experiences we thought would give us the freedom, pleasure, or satisfaction we expected, end up enslaving us. Everything we buy, whether small or large, can set a hook into our minds and our souls. When we follow our plan instead of God's plan—or, more accurately, when we take control instead of surrendering to God—we make choices that are weakening our financial futures.

- *Write down three financial choices you are making right now. Who is winning control over those decisions? You or God?*

- *If you are putting your plans ahead of God's plans, describe some of the likely future outcomes with your spouse, your family, or your job, if you continue following your path.*

- *Write Matthew 6:19-21.*

2 As we may desire our resources to increase, we can grab the steering wheel away from God, feeling He is not delivering fast enough and doesn't know what we really need.

- *What is the worst financial decision you ever made? What does that experience teach you about the triggers that tend to motivate our financial decisions?*

- *What message hit your trigger? How do you recognize the message that has the potential to hit that same trigger again?*

- *Write 1 John 4:1.*

3 After tempting you with the very thing (or things) he knows you want, the enemy then often distracts you from enjoying it. These things create barriers between you and God and potentially between you and your spouse.

- Share some real examples of how you have experienced conflict in your relationships over money related choices?

- Have you ever purchased an item you wanted, of any size, that later caused a wedge in your marriage?

- What did you do about it? How was it resolved?

- Write Jeremiah 29:11.

4 A little distraction is all it takes. A little lie from the world instead of truth from God. The truth that everything we need comes from Him and belongs to Him. And everything means everything. As we move farther along in our plan, traps set by the enemy can distract us from God's plans. Sometimes, we build barriers with the very resources He gave us to honor Him and use for His plans.

- *What have you built or created that you feel may have become a barrier to your faith and your relationship with God? What should you do about it?*

- *Describe a trap you may have experienced. How were you able to get out? Now that you know the trap, what does it look like to avoid a similar trap in the future?*

- *Is there a familiar whisper or common "bait" that leads you to make financial choices that have the capacity to move you away from God? Name a few.*

- *Write James 4:7.*

5 A lot of people confuse stewardship with tithing and think they are free to use their 90% as they see fit as long as they are giving their 10%. But since reports state that the average Christian gives only around 3% of their income, that means we are running at a 97% overhead! We've heard it so many times that it all comes from God and all is His. Yet, our lives and our giving usually don't reflect that.

- Consider all God has blessed you with. How are you using what He has entrusted to you in a way that honors Him?

- If not, where are you falling short and how can you correct it?

- If you are in a position to have more than you need, what are you doing with the more—the surplus?

- Write Colossians 3:23.

> *Stewardship is every choice you make after you've said **yes** to Jesus.*

6 Excess wealth without God's instructions, usually accelerates existing weaknesses. When you take control rather than submit to God's plan, you may have chosen to serve money, things, and stuff—and money makes a lousy savior. Money promises much but delivers little.

- *List some financial goals and some examples of how you may be placing too much trust in money to be the solution?*

- *What are you getting from your money that you should be getting from God?*

- *Write 1 Timothy 6:18-19.*

7 When we looked at the Cross Paradigm in the book, we learned how some, or all, of its characteristics affect your financial choices in one way or another. Reaching your financial goals only satisfy if those goals include being obedient to Christ.

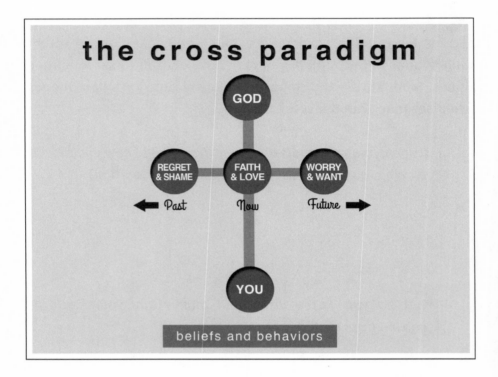

We tend to allow the regret and shame of the past and the worry and want of the future to take our eyes off of God and what He has planned for us. Add to that our long held beliefs and financial behaviors and we begin asking for things and making choices that aren't really what we need because they are skewed by those silent partners—worry & want, regret & shame, my perspective, my beliefs and behaviors.

- Use a money moment below, or choose your own, and describe how the Silent Partners from The Cross Paradigm may have impact on your approach to the moment and your final choice? Refer back to Week 1, Question #8, for some reminders. . .

- What would happen if we were to cover all of these moments in a living faith every day? Would these still have their power over us? Can these Silent Partners exist with a vibrant, living faith?

- **SAMPLE Money Moments:** Major purchase (car, home, etc.), Planning for retirement, allowances for your children, or other. . .

Money Moment	
What's my perspective?	
What's my belief?	
What's my behavior?	
What are my future desires?	
What are my past regrets?	
What is God's persepective?	

- Write Romans 12:2.

REFLECTION

Just as we tend to get a skewed perspective on what true freedom is, we often fail to grasp how freedom comes from releasing control in our lives and turning it over to God. Money truly is a lousy savior because it cannot deliver what it promises—it's a lie. It isn't reliable and it is only temporary—just like the world. It has no lasting or eternal power, but the power we give it tends to make us want to take control. This need to control our money and getting what we want in life is a major hurdle to living as God intended for us to live. When we insist on having things our way in our time, we don't leave God any room to work in our lives and we limit Him in what he is able to do for us. I can guarantee, His plan is bigger and more awesome than anything you or I can imagine. Our most perfect choice is placing our trust in Him and the plans He has for us, which results in the greatest of all freedoms.

MY PRAYER

Lord, I thought it would be different than this. I thought I could handle the tension and balancing act of my plans and your plans. From the outside, I may appear successful in many ways, yet what really matters has been steadily fading away. You designed me for dependence, and sometimes I act like I want to be on my own, but deep down that's not true. I only want to be on my own as long things are working out the way I want them. As soon as they don't, I want your help and want you in charge again. I know that's not the way it's supposed to be. I know it and you know it. Help me want you more than I want my worldly ways. Let my life reflect you. Please lead me along your path. Lord please let me rest in you and your perfect plans. Amen.

MY PRAYERS
+
PRAYER REQUESTS

n o t e s

notes

week **four**

[
we're not alone
+
less is more
]

Some of us were raised not to talk about money. Even for younger generations, when it comes to talking about mistakes in handling our personal finances, no one wants to talk. Whether it is because we are compelled to keep up the façade that we are better off than we really are, or just the embarrassment of making foolish choices, the collective silence makes us feel as though we are the only ones in the struggle. Plus, this makes the enemy's job easier when we remain isolated. This week we are opening up about this issue and looking more closely at what God wants us to know about money. We will learn where to find effective support. And we will discover that few have as much as they'd like everyone to believe and that's actually okay because less is more in God's economy.

(Psalm 33:10-15)
(John 3:30-31)

1 When things aren't going so well in our financial lives, we can avoid the subject of money and we start thinking we're the only ones in trouble. Feeling and remaining isolated in our frustration over money inhibits our heart's desire to love and serve God more fully and gives the enemy a clear shot at our hearts.

- *How has keeping your financial fears private kept you from serving God effectively?*

- *Describe the blessing of being able to openly pray together with your spouse and let your feelings be known.*

- *Can you share how you pray together and what it means to your marriage?*

- *Write Matthew 18:19.*

2 Those we worship with on Sunday morning are likely wrestling with financial distractions as well, though like us, they have become quite skillful at hiding their pain and the impact on their life and marriage. Some people are dealing with the distraction of abundance and others with distraction of scarcity and neither have their full focus on God. While there are certain aspects of your finances that may not be appropriate to share in public, finding others in a similar situation, or sharing with wise private counsel, allows you to gain perspective.

- *List some positive things can you learn from knowing you are not alone in your journey?*

- *What can you learn about the true nature of God's blessing from this?*

- *Do you feel God leading you to share a financial pain with your group? What about with private counsel, or one of The Seven?*

-Write Psalm 23:1.

3 The money mirage isn't a new phenomenon. Lots of people in the Bible made the same choices you've made, though they didn't necessarily live a joyful life. If trusting money and things instead of God weren't universal temptations, the Bible wouldn't have so much to say about it. God also knew the power of the enemy's whisper to gradually pull us away from Him by using money as a trap.

- What is the best financial advice you have ever received and where did it come from?

- Does that best advice agree or disagree with what God tells us in Scripture about handling money?

- *What is the best scriptural financial advice you ever received? How has it helped you? Has it ever been wrong?*

- *Write 2 Timothy 3:16-17.*

4 Remember, what God wants more than anything is to have a relationship with you, and that's difficult if you are wrapped up in obtaining and maintaining. Think about your typical quiet time with God—prayer, scripture, journaling, etc.

- *How satisfied are you with how this has been going? Explain.*

- *What kinds of things tend to interfere with ability to spend time with God?*

- Identify one change you could realistically make to improve your time with God and minimize interferences.

- Write 1 Thessalonians 5:16-18.

5 *The Seven* are God-given resources around you where you can turn for guidance and support at any time and have confidence in them. However, few of us make a point to develop and utilize them so they are there when we need them most. The benefits of *The Seven* are powerful in your life.

- Beside each one write down how you believe it will make an impact on your financial choices.

1. Prayer
Write Matthew 6:6.

2. God's Word
Write Matthew 24:35.

3. Your Spouse
Write Genesis 2:24.

4. Close Friend
Write James 5:16.

5. Godly Counsel
Write Proverbs 24:6.

6. Your Pastor
Write Jeremiah 3:15.

7. God's Church.
Write Ephesians 2:21-22.

- *Take a moment and write down how you will incorporate The Seven and the individuals that you believe will fill these Godly positions in your life.*

6 Whatever worries you face, or that wake you up at night, are not bigger than the God who loves you. As you grow in the knowledge of how to honor God with your finances and in your relationship with Him, one of the greatest gifts you can give back to Him is how you see yourself fitting in to someone else's *Seven*.

- *What insights, wisdom, or experiences do you have right now that would be beneficial to another?*

- *Who in your circle of family, friends, or co-workers might you be able to reach out to and offer your support?*

- Write Ecclesiastes 4:9-12.

7 If in God's plan "less is more", and if you desire to abandon your plan for His, let's talk about what that mean in practical terms.

- List three things you can do to create "less world" in your life?

- List three things you can do to create "more God" in your life?

- Set a date when you will take steps to create both of those prior lists and identify one of The Seven who will encourage you and hold you accountable.

- Write Philippians 3:7.

REFLECTION

We all tend to build and spend and cling to our plan instead of trusting God because we fear His plan isn't going to cover our needs (which also includes our wants). Many times we become isolated and confused in our struggles because we don't realize others are facing similar problems and no one is talking about it. Pride and other dangerous feelings can creep in which makes us become even more private with our money choices. Having a support system for all aspects of our lives is important. Having resources, friends and wise counsel to turn to for guidance in navigating the tough life questions is vital. If you are feeling alone, you are more prone to making poor choices and more prone to listen to the whisper of the enemy. Learning to trust God in this area is not easy, but opening up and talking with others, developing *The Seven*, and spending time with God will strengthen you faith and with that, your financial choices.

PRAYER

You chose the twelve to accompany you and learn from you. At the perfect time you sent them out in pairs to strengthen, challenge and pray for each other as they became your apostles. They had so little yet lived so richly. I have so much and feel alone. I've let my pride get in the way of my transparency with my spouse and those who love me. I'm tired and I know I need the kind of rest that can only be found in You and received from those who love You. I know that I need You and Your wisdom. I need to clear away and open wide the space between us. Help me recognize those resources You have placed around me to guide me in Your way. Help me to know You will always be all I will ever need. Amen.

MY PRAYERS
+
PRAYER REQUESTS

notes

n o t e s

week **five**

We've chipped away at our money moments and financial decisions and what is behind them. We've unpacked the needs, the wants, the misconceptions, and the internal and external influences driving the choices that can get us into messes. Now we get to look at what comes next and how you can move forward in God's plans and more of His blessing. To strip away the power of money and use it as a tool. We will explore how to re-strengthen your relationships with your spouse, and God, to be healthy and strong. God wants us here, focused on today, yet open to Him and where He wants to take us. The choice to follow God more closely is available to each of us every moment of every day. And now it's time for focused action. Let's have some fun.

(2 Corinthians 5:11-16)
(2 Corinthians 5:17-21)

1 Physically, financially, and materially—you will build barriers, traps will be set for you, and you will encounter hazards in your path. When you slip, get up, brush yourself off, and keep moving forward. Remember, the goal is progress, not perfection. Progress happens on earth, perfection only happens in Heaven.

- Instead of getting frustrated when you have missteps, list a few ways to get back on track. Is there a recent memory?

- Write 1 John 1:9.

2 The key is wanting more of God than what the world offers. You will find that your money issues will also begin to diminish when you focus on living in God's provision rather than your own. The steps you have begun to take will reward you with the joy that God has always wanted for you and a peace that emanates from His spirit deep within you.

- Make a list of reminders of all the ways God is providing His blessings for you. Be specific. Use this as a reference when you begin doubting. Add to the list as you see more of His provision.

- Write Philippians 4:19.

3 In Chapter 9 of the book, I shared a powerful exercise called *Finding Your Now. (If you haven't finished it yet, please take time to do that now.)* I walked you through *The Stewardship Question* (Financial SQ) which helps you envision your near future, yet focuses on today's activities to live more in tune with God and His plans for you. Then we spent time completing the *Financial Four Helpful Lists* (Financial 4HL) that takes a dynamic inventory of your financial status. Once completed, you narrowed this down to a list of *MUST DOs*, then placed each of those into the *ReNew Filter* (RF) and peeled away the layers of the task to gain clarity and unity of the action at hand. Finally, you narrowed those filtered tasks further to a *Prayer & Action* list of two to three tasks.

- *In the introduction I spoke about an open oneness in community with each other. If you feel God leading you, share your #1 MUST DO that God revealed to you and the ReNew Filter details. Be courageous! Comment on both the anticipated spiritual growth and financial results.*

- *Write Hebrews 12:1.*

4 God wants you content in only Him and honoring Him with your life. By consciously choosing to discard the stuff and activities that tie us to this world, we're going to make room for God to operate in our lives.

- *If time or money were not an issue, name three things that you would love to do today that would fall under the category of loving God or loving others?*

- *If you have ever thought about downsizing in areas of your life, what appeals to you? What frightens or concerns you? Be bold and specific.*

- *Write 2 Corinthians 8:12.*

5 We want the abundant life that comes from loving God and others, but the lifestyle that we have built may not let us have it. Some of the tallest barriers to God have been built by us and we can be pretty proud of our accomplishments.

- *What are some barriers that you have erected that can interfere between you and God?*

- *What would God's best look like if you begin to dismantle that barrier?*

- Write Leviticus 26:1.

6 "Sometimes you have to change your playground and your playmates." (And I think many of us may have to swap out our toys as well!)

- In order for you to pack light, what would be the first three things each of you would jettison?

- Write Isaiah 43:18-19.

7 When you look and pack more like the disciples, your minimal stuff does not become a drain on resources and there is less time devoted to caring for it. You can make adjustments quickly, you have more freedom from your finances, and less distraction for the plans God has in store.

- *How would it feel for you to be free enough to move toward God whenever you sensed God leading you into a new adventure— to be able to drop what you were doing and just go?*

- *If you both had to take a prayerfully educated guess at His plans for you, where might he be leading? Be courageous to share what He has put on your heart.*

- *Write Ephesians 2:10.*

8 Choosing God, and God alone, in abundance or in scarcity, will allow you to live for free in that peaceful place where God is your only desire and money is only another resource used to honor Him.

- *Whether you're on that journey now, or if you are ready to take that journey with God, you will have to take a first step. What is yours?*

- Use the space below to write a commitment to yourself and to God to trust Him to lead you to live for free.

- Write Proverbs 3:5-6.

May the God of hope fill you with all joy and peace as you trust in Him, so that you may overflow with hope by the power of the Holy Spirit.
-Romans 15:13

REFLECTION

Our financial choices are a window into who we are, what we believe, and who or what we trust. Stewardship isn't just about being obedient to God by only tithing or giving of your time and talents to Him. It is about honoring God in how you use all of the resources provided for you to accomplish all of the plans God has for the world. It truly is every choice you make after you say yes to Jesus. By reconnecting with God through these exercises and reacquainting yourself with the purpose He has for you, you can recapture your life. We do equate money with freedom, but we're designed to equate freedom with God. As you journey toward this redefined financial freedom, you will be more prepared to make the right choice in whom you will trust and who will be your guide on the journey. Money will become just another resource in your plan aimed at Heaven. God wants you and you alone. God wants you to live for free.

PRAYER

Lord, how I want to rely on your truths! I'm working so hard but I don't seem to be getting anywhere. I can't keep up with the world. It's moving too fast. I'm afraid sometimes that if I slow down, I'll get swept away. Maybe that's exactly what I need to do—to stop chasing after the world and let myself get swept away by you. You promise to catch me. You promise to be there. You promise me life that is truly life. Thank you for the hope and confidence you give us to know You and worship You. You allow us to make our own choices but You never stop loving us. You let us travel our own paths, knowing sometimes that they are taking us further from You, yet you faithfully wait for us. Forgive us for the times where we took advantage of Your love and forgiveness. Will you let us start together with you yet one more time? Will you free us of any distractions between us? Give us Your wisdom and the courage to follow You and live for free. Lord, You are the beginning and the end of every journey. Will You lead us toward the garden once again? Amen.

MY PRAYERS
+
PRAYER REQUESTS

n o t e s

n o t e s

it's not about the money.

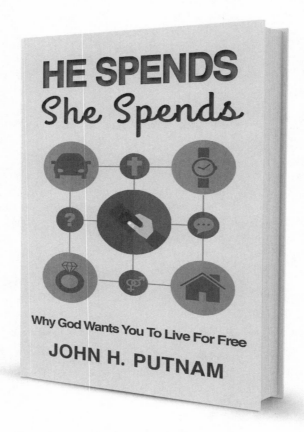

HE SPENDS
She Spends

Why God Wants You To Live For Free

JOHN H. PUTNAM

This book is a "why to" book rather than a "how to" book. After seeing and personally making more finacial mistakes than most people will experience, John H. Putnam shares what he's learned through his own walk with Christ, his personal financial journey, and what he's observed from working with families and individuals for over twenty-two years as a financial advisor. Because If we aim our hearts, our lives, and our resources at God, it might just give us the best chance to live like heaven right here on earth and find freedom in Christ rather than in our money.

Read an excerpt from this book and more at www.JohnHPutnam.com.

ABOUT THE AUTHOR

John H. Putnam has been married to Anne for twenty-seven years and has three incredible children. For more than twenty of those years, he had a thriving financial services practice advising individuals and families through thousands of conversations and thoughtful processes. As an avid writer, speaker, radio and television personality, he has shared his opinions, ideas and insights with millions of people on the financial issues they face. In 2005, John began to focus more on his clients' life planning and the unique perspectives behind their financial choices and spent years of concentrated study in this unique stewardship field. Throughout his journey, John has become increasingly intentional to help individuals and couples create spiritual clarity, unity, and context in their financial lives as they move toward achieving their Kingdom goals and impact, and now wants to help you do the same.